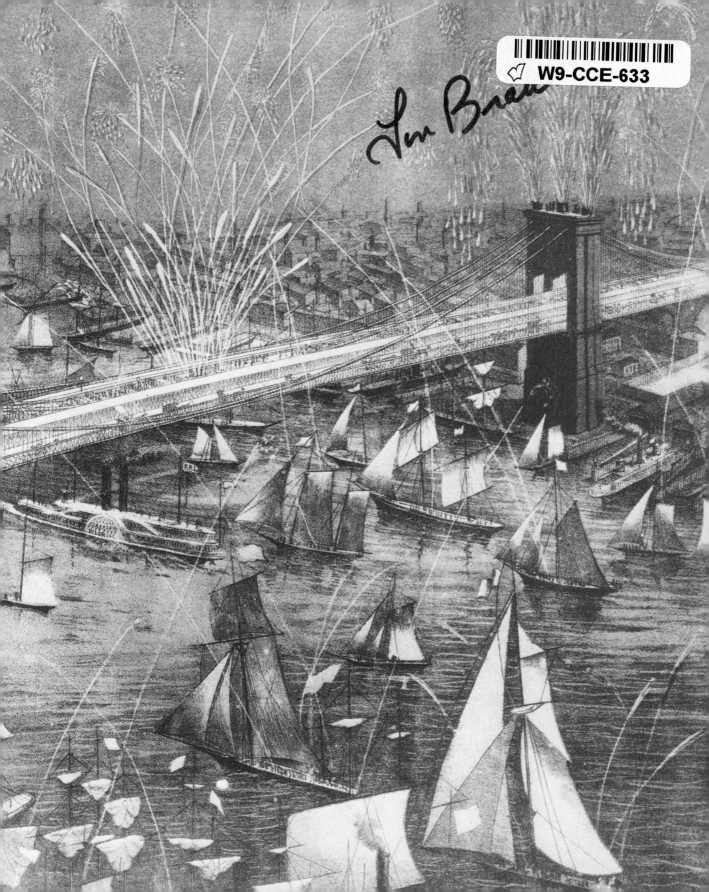

Let's Get Lost in a Painting

JOSEPH STELLA
The Brooklyn Bridge

by

**ROBERT J. SAUNDERS
AND ERNEST GOLDSTEIN**

designed by Marsha Cohen

Garrard Publishing Company
Champaign, Illinois

Dedicated to the memory of

George R. Saunders,

Structural Engineer and Brother.

Robert Saunders, Series Consultant

Diagram concepts by Robert Saunders

Drawings by Marsha Cohen

Library of Congress Cataloging in Publication Data

Goldstein, Ernest, 1933–
   Joseph Stella, the Brooklyn Bridge.

   (Let's get lost in a painting)
   Summary: Analyzes artist Joseph Stella's six paintings of
the Brooklyn Bridge, as well as some of his other works, and
depicts other artists' renditions of the famous bridge over the
East River.
   1. Stella, Joseph, 1877–1946–Juvenile literature. 2. Brooklyn Bridge (New York, N.Y.) in art—Juvenile literature. [1.
Brooklyn Bridge (New York, N.Y.) in art.
2. Stella, Joseph, 1877–1946. 3. Bridges in art.
4. Painting, American. 5. Art appreciation] I. Title. II. Series:
Goldstein, Ernest, 1933–   . Let's get lost in a painting.
ND237.S685G6 1984   759.13   84-10230
ISBN 0-8116-1006-3

Editorial and Production services by Cobb/Dunlop, Inc.

Manufactured in the United States of America.

Photo Acknowledgments

Currier and Ives *The Great East River Suspension Bridge*
The New York Historical Society
Page 1

Joseph Stella *The Bridge, The Voice of the City: New York Interpreted* (1922)
Collection of The Newark Museum
Page 5, Detail Page 7

John A. Roebling *(3) Drawings for the Brooklyn Bridge*
Rensselaer Polytechnic Institute Archives
Page 9

Richard Benson *Photograph of the Brooklyn Bridge* (1930)
Reproduced by permission of The Limited Editions Club
Page 10

Joseph Stella *The Croatian* (1908)
Hirshorn Museum and Sculpture Garden, Smithsonian Institute
Detail Page 19

Childe Hassam *Brooklyn Bridge in Winter* (1904)
Telfair Academy of Arts and Sciences, Inc.
Page 21

Albert Gleizes *On Brooklyn Bridge* (1917)
Collection of the Solomon R. Guggenheim Museum
Page 26

Joseph Stella *The Brooklyn Bridge* (1917–1918)
Yale University Art Gallery. Gift of Collection Société Anonyme
Page 29, Detail Page 31

Joseph Stella *The Voice of the City: New York Interpreted* (1922)
Collection of The Newark Museum
Page 32

Joseph Stella *American Landscape* (1929)
Collection of Walker Art Center. Gift of T. B. Walker Foundation
Page 37

Joseph Stella *The Bridge* (1936)
San Francisco Museum of Modern Art. WPA Federal Arts
Project, allocation to San Francisco Museum of Art
Page 39

Joseph Stella *Brooklyn Bridge, Variations on an Old
Theme* (1939)
Whitney Museum of American Art
Page 40

Joseph Stella *The Old Bridge* (1941)
Museum of Fine Arts, Boston. Lent by Susan Morse Hilles
Page 41

End Papers

Brooklyn Bridge - 1883 - *Fireworks at the Opening, May 24*
J. Clarence Davies Collection, Museum of the City of New
York

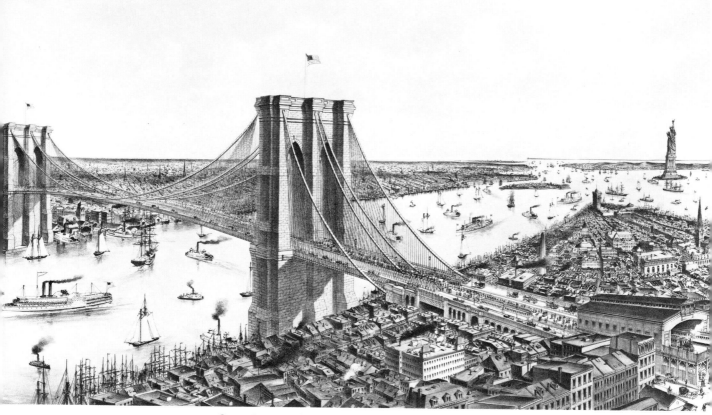

Currier and Ives *The Great East River Suspension Bridge*

From time immemorial bridges have excited, mystified, and even terrified the human imagination. In many ancient myths when a bridge was built, the river gods required a human sacrifice. In overcoming a natural water barrier, man had dared to change the landscape and defy the laws of nature. For such feats the river gods demanded their price.

Before New York City's Brooklyn Bridge was completed in 1883, it had already become a modern myth. During its construction, John Roebling, the designer and chief engineer, died from a freak accident on a pier. His son, Washington Roebling, continued his work and completed the bridge. During the construction he too had a mishap which left him paralyzed.

The Brooklyn Bridge took fourteen years to build. During that time the newspapers were filled with stories of scandal, corruption, and the deaths of workers. The idea of such a huge undertaking staggered the imagination. The Brooklyn Bridge would be larger than the Egyptian pyramids and the biggest structure ever built in America. Little was known of the genius and vision of John Roebling—or the dedication of his son Washington. But the public imagination had been stirred. Who was this lunatic Roebling, sitting paralyzed at his desk, field glasses in hand, directing the work below?

The Brooklyn Bridge was officially opened in 1883. Chester A. Arthur, President of the United States, led the first walk across. To the many speakers at the opening dedication, the Brooklyn Bridge was a look into the future—a victory for American science and technology. For the first time, steel had replaced iron. The use of cables changed forever the method of building suspension bridges. And wonder of wonders, light was coming from Thomas Edison's marvelous new invention, the electric lamp!

Besides benefiting business and commerce, the Brooklyn Bridge was a "people's bridge." The main riverspan of 1600 feet over the New York Harbor had two levels. Roadways on the lower level were for trains, wagons, and horse-drawn carriages. Above the roadways was one of John Roebling's ingenious ideas—a promenade for walkers.

The public celebrated the opening in grand style, with parties, dancing and fireworks throughout the night. On Memorial Day 1883, a week after the opening, another incident added to the myth of the Brooklyn Bridge. As thousands strolled along the promenade, a voice cried out: "The bridge is falling!" Panic followed. In the rush to escape, twelve people were trampled to death. It was the dawn of a new age and the river gods had claimed more victims.

When the bridge opened it joined two separate cities: New York and Brooklyn. Fifteen years later, Brooklyn

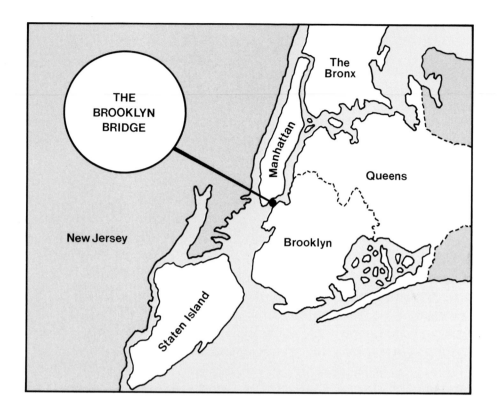

became a borough of New York, adding approximately one million people to the city. New York City is now composed of five boroughs: Manhattan, Brooklyn, Queens, the Bronx, and Staten Island. The map shows all five boroughs and the location of the Brooklyn Bridge.

Much has happened to New York City in the last one hundred years, and the Brooklyn Bridge has had an important role in the change. John Roebling's prophecy of "millions of people crossing the bridge" has been fulfilled. On the lower level automobiles and trucks have replaced the horse, but on the promenade pedestrians still enjoy the breathtaking "path to the stars." For over one hundred years this awesome miracle of technology has cast a spell on the human imagination. It's been painted, drawn, and photographed more than any other bridge in the world. Poets compose poems about it. Authors write about it. Playwrights write plays that take place in its shadows. In movies spies whisper and lovers stroll on it. Travelers and tourists from all parts of the world go to see it. It is as much a part of the natural landscape as Niagara Falls or the Grand Canyon. In a sense it is more. Designed by the German-born John Roebling, built by the sweat of immigrant workers, and facing the Statue of Liberty, the Brooklyn Bridge has become a universal symbol of America's experience, achievement, and dreams.

To the artist Joseph Stella the Brooklyn Bridge was a national shrine and a personal obsession. Obsessions are thoughts which will not leave the mind. Stella's obsession with the bridge—its history and design—led him to live near it, walk on it often, make countless sketches and six large paintings of it. His 1922 painting (his second painting of the bridge) is a landmark work in the history of modern art in America. Before looking at Stella's bridge, go back to the map of New York and the photographs of the bridge. Locate Manhattan, Brooklyn, and the bridge. Then go to the painting. Do you recognize it as the Brooklyn Bridge? How? Try to determine where you are standing on Stella's bridge.

At first glance, the pointed arches suggest a doorway instead of a bridge. If it is a bridge, where is the part that goes over the river and what are those long white strips hanging down? The pointed arches are the doorways of the bridge. You walk through them when you enter or leave it. Stella chose to paint the arches and the tower. He included the four main cables (the long white strips) and the city beyond. But where is the riverspan—the part that goes across the river? It is there, but can you find it?

That's right—you are standing on it, suspended over the river. This is the artist's point of view—the place from which Stella looks at the bridge. The artist and the viewer are in the middle of the bridge looking at the tower. From this position, the eye level is halfway up the

Joseph Stella *The Bridge* (1922)

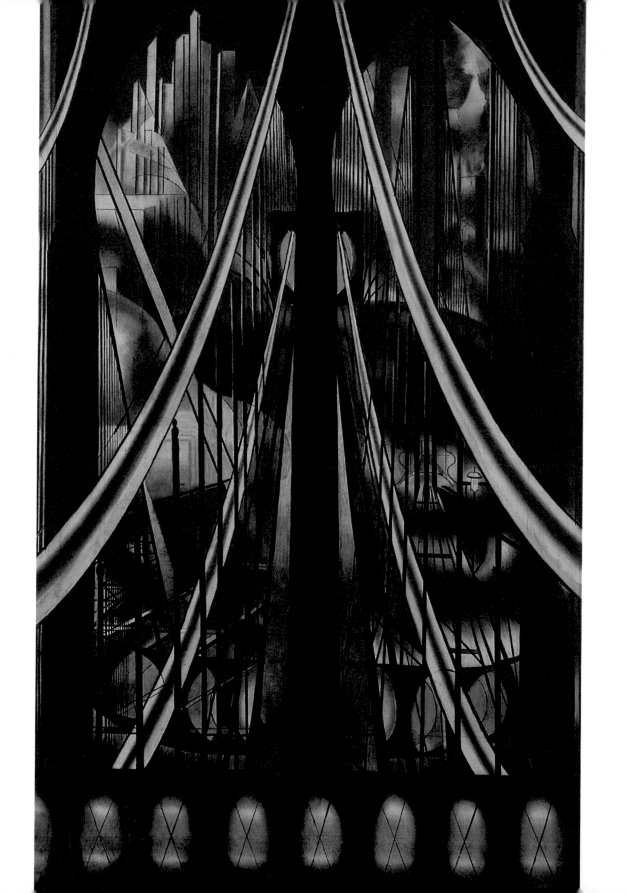

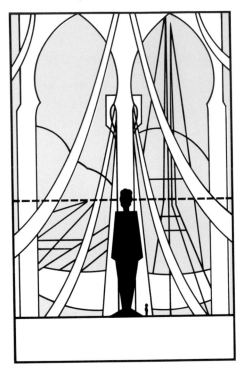

The *eye-level line* is an imaginary line showing where the eye spans when looking straight ahead. It moves higher and lower as the eye moves higher and lower.

tower. The drawing shows the eye-level line of the painting.

Stella plays tricks with the eye-level line in order to see the bridge his way. The arches soar 105 feet above the walkway. We would have to be about 55 feet tall to see from an eye level that high. If he had made the view 5 or 6 feet high, the eye level would be approximately that of the small figure in the drawing. We would not see very much and the height of the towers would overpower us. Standing on the promenade, we would also not see what is underneath. So Stella gave the viewer x-ray eyes, showing the roadway with cars and flashing headlights under the walkway. The understructure of the bridge— the I-beams and arches of steel braces and supports—are all part of Stella's story, so he placed them in the very center of the painting.

Stella's bridge had two different worlds. At night he often walked alone on the promenade. He heard the wind hum through the cables and the sound of the traffic below. He saw moving headlights flashing through the structure and plankings. The quiet space and distant stars seen from the promenade were far different from the view on the lower level. That was a ferocious, frantic world of rushing traffic and the deafening whine of tires on steel gratings. The noise filled the air around the bridge like a dense cloud. What the eye did not see, the ear could hear from that position on the promenade. He paints the noise with color and line. The red, blues, and greens in the corner angles and grid work below the eye level, in the lower half of the painting, describe the hub-bub of the lower roadway. Across the bottom, a row of oval lights suggests the tunnels and subways below the bridge under the East River.

By looking at the photograph, can you tell on which end of the bridge you are standing? At which tower you are looking? There are two main clues. The first is the skyscrapers beyond the tower. Those tall buildings can only be the Manhattan skyline. The second clue is the small square shape midway up the central column in the painting. The detail shows the Manhattan Tower.

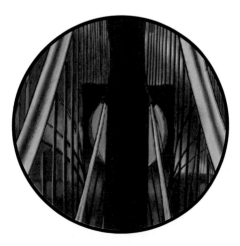

The arches in front are in the Brooklyn Tower. Stella painted the bridge from the Brooklyn side with Manhattan in the background. His Manhattan is not a real city. None of the buildings is recognizable. It is a fantasy city. The buildings are not steel, stone, or glass. They are thin lines with flickering shadows passing over pale walls above dark blue and gray clouds of smoke and fog. Stella's buildings float in air and do not rest firmly on the bedrock of Manhattan.

Let's go back to 1922, the year of Stella's painting. He called his work simply *The Bridge.* Most people even if they were not familiar with New York immediately recognized *The Bridge* as the Brooklyn Bridge. Why?

The answer is the boardwalk and the arches of the towers. The Brooklyn Bridge is the only bridge in the world with a promenade deck where people can walk and sit on benches and with two Gothic arches in each tower. These arches are high and narrow, with a point at the top of the curve. They are called "Gothic" after a style of architecture used in great stone cathedrals built several hundred years ago in Europe. The Gothic style revolutionized architecture by creating soaring height and an appearance of lightness. In the 1840s Gothic architecture became popular in America. This style was the proper choice for the bridge with which Roebling was to revolutionize American engineering. Since the Gothic style gives the feeling of height, it suited Roebling's purpose for "his cathedral to the stars." That Roebling was aware of the importance of his monument can be seen from his different drawings for the towers. He first designed Egyptian-style towers, then round Roman arches which he finally changed to Gothic arches.

By 1922, most of the world was familiar with these arches. The title *The Bridge* could only have meant the Brooklyn Bridge. People knew it even if they did not understand the painting.

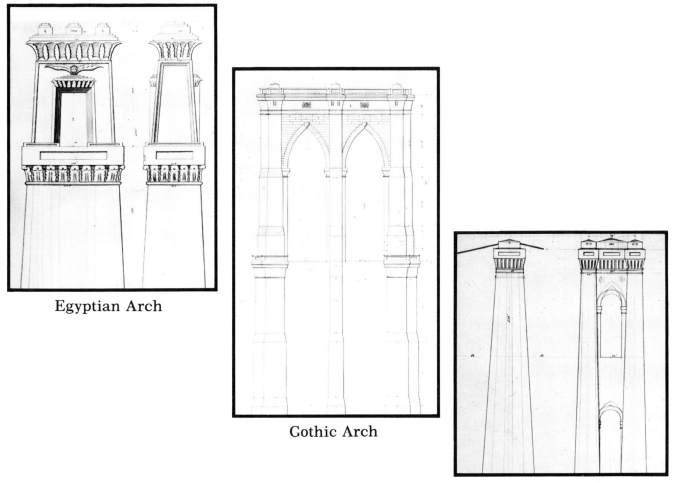

Egyptian Arch

Gothic Arch

Roman Arch

They might have understood a photograph more easily. In a photograph, at least everything is where one expects to see it. The photograph taken by Richard Benson for Hart Crane's famous poem "The Bridge" (1930) is a good example. Crane had seen Stella's painting and the photograph suggests that the photographer might also have seen it. The photograph is a more accurate picture than Stella's painting. But Stella was saying something about the bridge that a photograph can't say. (page 10)

Both pictures show the arches, but the photograph also shows the whole tower and the sky and buildings on both sides of it. Both pictures show the steel ropes. In the

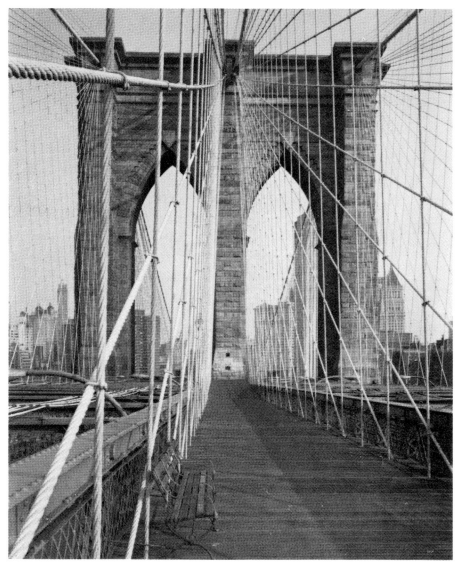

Richard Benson *Photograph of the Brooklyn Bridge* (1930)

photograph the steel ropes are like a spider's web or a net because the shot includes the diagonal ropes. The painting shows only the vertical steel ropes (not the diagonal ropes), and it also includes the four long white cable casings. The four main cables are too high above the camera's eye level to be captured in the photograph. The photograph shows the cables lying over the roadway on each side of the boardwalk, but it cannot show us the roadway underneath. Stella could select the parts of the bridge he wanted in his painting, and leave out the parts he did not want. Benson could select which view he wanted, how close to get to the towers, how far to the left or the right on the boardwalk, and the direction in which to point the lens. He could control the light, the shutter speed, and the focus. But he could not change the shadows; he could only wait for the sun to do that. His camera eye level was only three or four feet from the boardwalk.

The drawing below shows where Benson stood to shoot his photograph. Notice how far away he is from the tower and how low the camera eye level is. Compare it with the drawing on page 6 of the eye level in the painting.

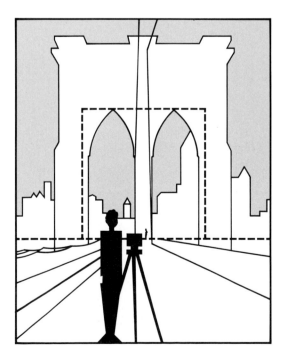

In the drawing of Benson's photograph the dotted line around the arches is the portion of the bridge which Stella uses in his painting. Notice how few of the buildings are visible inside the arches of the photograph. Benson's photograph shows the Manhattan skyline of 1930. Stella's painting of 1922 shows buildings that had not yet been built. His skyline is more like that of today than that of 1922. The camera can capture only what is there and what the photographer chooses to focus on. Stella painted what the camera cannot see. That is one difference between a photograph and a painting. Each requires a well-trained eye and a special kind of imagination. The artist and the photographer must be able to visualize what the finished picture will be. Each looked for the truth of the bridge as he imagined it. But which one shows the true bridge?

There is no one answer. The bridge has as many truths as there are creative artists. To the writer Henry James the bridge was a "mechanical spider" working on the sky. The line in Hart Crane's poem "unspeakable thou Bridge to thee, O love" tells of a poet's freedom when he walked the bridge to escape the city. What was Roebling's truth? What was Stella's truth? The answer to the first question sheds light on the second.

For years the citizens of Manhattan and Brooklyn had wanted and needed a bridge. In winter when the water froze, travel and commerce were almost impossible. Have times changed? Over 100 years ago, *The New York Times* felt the bridge could reduce two major problems: crime and overcrowding! Bridge engineers had submitted many plans but the problems could not be solved. The East River's currents were difficult and tricky. The river had some of the busiest boat traffic in the world and federal law required that a bridge not interfere with navigation. A bridge would have to be built high above the water and ground level of both cities. The task seemed impossible. Roebling's solution was a suspension bridge with two stone towers (The "Manhattan tower" on one side and the "Brooklyn tower" on the other) resting on the solid bedrock of the river bottom. The drawing shows the two stone towers and the principle of a suspension bridge.

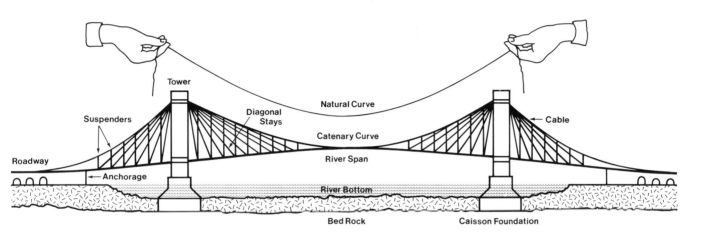

Roebling's design was a symbol of perfect balance when natural forces are at rest. The "natural forces" were the weight of the towers (the force of gravity) against the natural curve of the cables. Four main cables suspended between the towers supported the riverspan from vertical steel ropes called suspenders. These cables formed a natural curve in the way the rope curves between the two hands in the diagram.

At such a height a powerful wind could raise and twist such a long riverspan. So Roebling designed a series of radiating steel ropes called stays that cross and are clamped to each of the suspenders. Together the stays and tower (or suspenders) and riverspan form right triangles.

The relaxed natural curve of the cables and the strength of the right triangles represented natural forces at rest. The recognition of the geometrical forces in nature was a mathematical principle discovered by the ancient Greek philosopher Pythagoras. Roebling used it for his bridge.

In the Benson photograph you saw and immediately recognized the bridge. Not so in Stella's painting. Part of the reason why Stella's bridge is difficult to identify is because it is an "abstract" work. The word "abstract" has challenged artists and critics, and to this day it has mystified the public. It has several different meanings. For our purposes, abstract literally means "to take out from." In abstract art the artist takes something out from the natural or "real" appearance of objects. In order to understand the abstract artist, we must look at his work with different eyes and a new attitude. We must experience it—perhaps even participate in it—before we recognize it. Instead of a "realistic" picture, Stella invites us to feel the height and symmetry of his bridge.

At the very first glance, we can feel the sweep and symmetry of Stella's "abstraction." The strong vertical lines of the arches create a sense of height and upward motion. Locate the promenade. Although horizontal, it has the appearance of being vertical. The promenade feels the way people first described it— as a "passageway to the stars."

How did Stella create his illusion of height? Go back to the painting again. Determine how the position of the towers, cables and vertical lines create height and balance.

The size is the first clue. *The Bridge* is a vertical painting, meaning that it is taller than it is wide. The three dominant vertical lines of the towers meet and push the eye upward to the pointed Gothic archways. Stella continues the vertical idea in the placement of the cables. The grand sweep of the three sets of cables look like steps pushing the eye ever upward (see diagram).

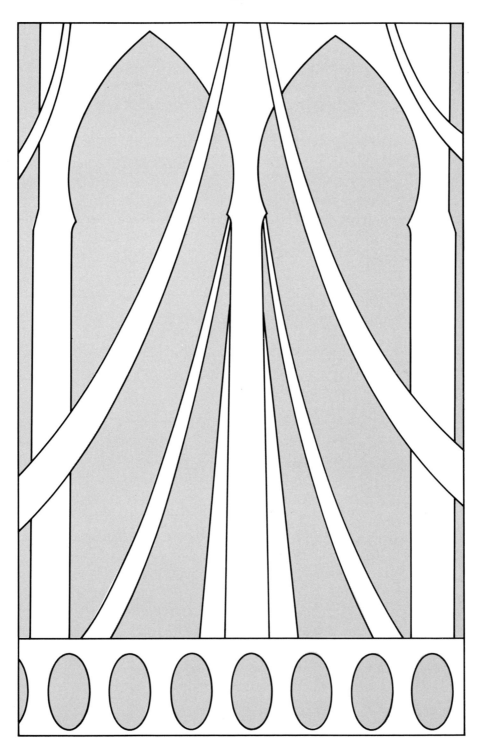

All this upward motion would make no visual sense if Stella did not balance the design and bring the eye to rest. Look at the arrangement in the diagram. The two Gothic arches have the shapes of bloated triangles. The three sets of cables meet to form triangles which create stability and symmetry. Symmetry means that both sides are equally balanced. The constant repetition of the triangles is called "triangulation." Roebling constructed his bridge around the principle of the right angle of triangles. Stella planned his painting around the isosceles triangle (a triangle that has two equal sides.) In this way he celebrated the triangulation of Roebling's design without copying it.

Right Triangle 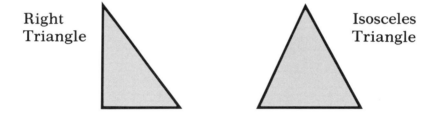 Isosceles Triangle

Stella's bridge is balanced and at rest. The triangles give the upward vertical movement a solid base. The bridge is symmetrical, but is the painting? Go one step beyond the bridge. Look through the archways. Decide if the painting is symmetrical.

At first glance the painting seems symmetrical, but that is an illusion. The major structures—the sets of cables and the archways create a symmetrical design. But inside the arches different things are happening. Through the left arch are the tall buildings of Manhattan; through the right are the heavy structure of the bridge and the lower roadway. The archways create a double image, as if one is a mirror of the other. Notice how he repeated the vertical buildings of the left archway in the vertical idea of the bridge in the right one. It is a visual trick. What is happening inside each archway is totally different. There are not one, but at least three separate stories: The drama and symmetry of the bridge, the distant buildings of the left portal, and the roadway underneath through the right.

In the archways, Stella created distance and depth. An artist shows distance by overlapping one object on another or by placing objects higher and smaller on the canvas. In the left archway the Manhattan skyline is the most distant part of the painting. Stella placed the buildings higher and smaller, overlapping other buildings and cloud shapes. The buildings are the most distant part of the painting. An artist shows depth by lines that converge to a point. Before going to the diagram, can you locate the deepest part of the painting (depth) in the right archway? (page 18)

Follow the lines of the roadway to the very end. The imaginary point where they meet takes you into the deepest part of Stella's space. The converging lines of the roadway create what is called in art the illusion of depth. You are standing on his bridge looking at the distant buildings. At the same time you are still inside the artist's space—feeling the life of a roadway you cannot actually see—even though you know it is there. At this point you are now lost in the artist's painting. If he has succeeded, you are everywhere at once—you feel the sensations of the vertical motion of the city, the frenzy of traffic on the road below—all framed by the heavy weight of the "abstract" symmetrical structure. Does it make any difference that Stella's painting is not a natural representation of a bridge? Probably not. Abstract art makes demands on the viewer. If you are willing to stay with the artist the word "abstract" is no longer a threat.

In 1922 Stella's *Bridge* was praised immediately. In time it was recognized as a landmark painting. It helped introduce abstract art in America. For Joseph Stella as

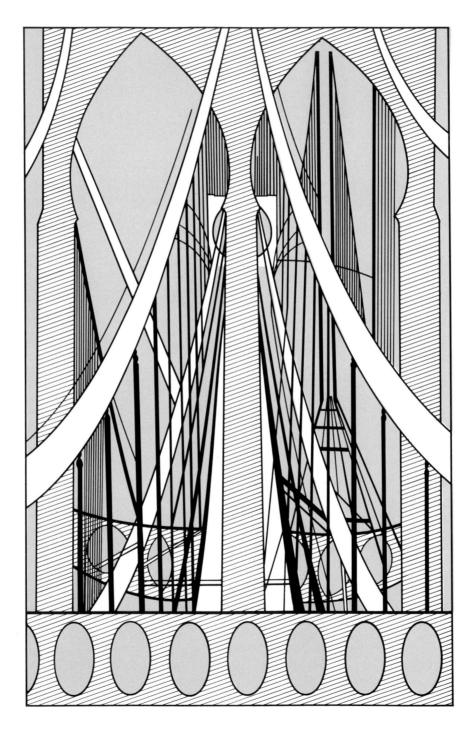

well as the general public, *The Bridge* was a leap into the 20th century. Until this work, Stella had been known mostly for his portraits of immigrants in New York City and his haunting drawings of life around the Pittsburgh steel mills. These he painted in a traditional style. In *The Bridge* he used a technique called Cubism to create the depth in the roadway. For Stella, an untrained artist, mastery of Cubism was a major achievement. And, as an Italian immigrant, Stella made another one by creating a universal symbol of American life. It took Stella 20 years from the first time he saw the bridge to paint it. During that time, he completed two educations: one as an artist, the other as an immigrant in New York City. From one he learned how to paint. From the other he learned what to see in the land of opportunity. He needed both educations to paint his bridge.

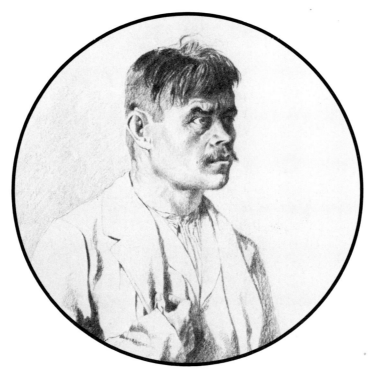

Joseph Stella *The Croatian* (1908)

Joseph Stella was born in 1879 in Muro Lucano, a small Italian village near Mt. Vesuvius, and received his education in nearby Naples. At the age of 19 he joined his brother on New York City's Lower East Side—a neighborhood inhabited mostly by immigrants. Although he had shown much artistic talent as a youngster, his father, a poor village lawyer, wanted Joseph to become a doctor. After one year of medical studies, the budding artist quit and in 1897 he enrolled in the Art Students' League of New York. Later he studied at the New York School of Art, where he came under the influence of an important American artist and a leader of the "Ash Can" School, Robert Henri.

At the beginning of the 20th century, revolutions were taking place against traditional ideas of art and beauty. One of these revolutions was the "Ash Can" School of art, so called because "ash can" artists painted everyday activities in the city streets. The Ash Can School showed a new idea of beauty that was really a new concept of truth. The paintings shocked a public used to the romantic paintings of the 19th century. People wanted their art to be pretty and expected to see happy portraits, still lifes, and peaceful landscapes. But times had changed— the Ash Can artists wanted to paint the world as they saw it. They saw an industrial world of factories and factory workers, a world of people on the streets, on rooftops, in restaurants, and in the theater. They painted the poor and the immigrants. It was a world of cities created by big business and industry.

The artist Childe Hassam painted the Brooklyn Bridge through the eyes of the Ash Can painters, although he was not considered one of them. His painting, *Brooklyn Bridge in Winter,* shown here, has certain features of the Ash Can style. It shows us a bleak city of buildings and rooftops heavy with dirty snow on a dismal day in 1904. Hassam painted it from a high point, probably

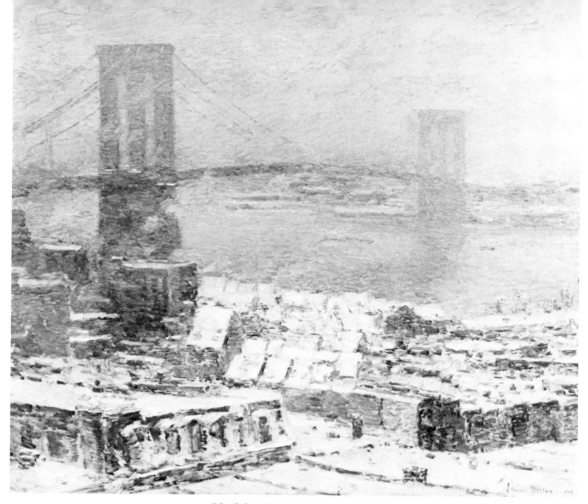

Childe Hassam *Brooklyn Bridge in Winter* (1904)

from a window above the other buildings. It is a long-distance view that includes both towers. The nearest tower is vague in the mist and smoke, but the distant tower is still more vague and lost. Hassam's painting also shows tenements crowded together in the part of the city where Stella lived (the Lower East Side of New York).

Joseph Stella was not one of the Ash Can painters, but he was a part of the Ash Can world. He came to America expecting to find New York City full of opportunity and the dreams of his favorite poet, Walt Whitman. Instead he found a city of dirty, crowded streets, walled in by tall buildings. He found himself imprisoned between dark tenements, under spider webs of clotheslines with laundry blocking out the sun. He walked about day and night with his pencil, charcoal and sketch pads, drawing his Italian immigrant neighbors. For a change of environment, he walked about Manhattan in the theater district and out on the Brooklyn Bridge to smell the clear air and feel open space around him.

The Ash Can painters made pictures of factories and immigrants popular in some magazines. As a result, Stella was hired between 1905 and 1907 to illustrate books about working people and about immigrants arriving at Ellis Island. Two assignments for *Survey Magazine* affected him the rest of his life. He went with a journalist to report on a mine disaster in Monogah, West Virginia. Almost the entire male working population was buried alive when the mines caved in. He sketched the grief and despair of the women, and the tragic weary faces of the men who lived only to become the grave diggers of the town. They dug out the bodies of their fathers, brothers, sons and friends only to dig again and bury them in graves. Stella's other assignment was in Pittsburgh. He drew the steel workers in factories, the miners, and families in the dark dank shacks they called home. He wrote later that he tried to show "the spasm and pathos of those workers condemned to a very strenuous life, exposed to the constant MENACE OF DEATH." Many drawings were of the huge monsters, the machines themselves. He had discovered the dark nightmare in the American dream. Out of all that power, force, and energy, coal and steel, smoke and noise, came giant buildings and bridges—as well as poverty, disaster and death.

In 1909 Stella returned to the warmth of his native Italy. There he visited the great museums and studied the glazing techniques of the Renaissance masters. But 14th- and 15th-century techniques were too slow and time-consuming for the emotions Stella wanted to express. One day when trying to paint a mountain outside Muro Lucano, he threw down his brushes. He was finished imitating the past. In 1911 Stella went to Paris to discover the art of his own time.

The Ash Can revolution in America was only a small part of a bigger revolution in the art world. Paris was the center of that revolution. Here in the early part of the 20th century modern art had its beginnings. Artists from all over the world came to Paris to look at the way Henri Matisse used colors and Pablo Picasso placed an object in space. These geniuses and their fellow artists were creating new ways of making paintings, new ways of seeing life. Modern art was not one but several revolutions going on at the same time. The word "modern" is difficult because it does not refer to time, such as the present. "Modern art" refers to the way artists were breaking away from a tradition of painting established by a thousand years of Western art. In the early 1900s artists began looking at the world with different eyes. Many of them were no longer interested in the natural appearance of life or things, what are called "realistic pictures." A camera could do that.

They were interested in going beyond a realistic picture to express something they saw in its color, shape or line, something a camera could not do. The motto for the modern artist came from Matisse when he said: "One must not imitate what one wants to create."

That statement meant different things to different artists. For Matisse the colors of a table could have their own personality. Matisse could paint a table with such power that the viewer might or might not recognize it until he felt the values and emotions of Matisse's color. Another modern artist might paint only the structure of the table by "abstracting" its lines, shapes or geometric pattern. A viewer might recognize it—again he might not—because the artist was making new demands. A third artist might ask the viewer to look at all sides of the table at the same time from different angles. A fourth or fifth artist might use combinations of these styles. In a sense this is not all that new; artists for thousands of years had "abstracted" by putting their feelings into the shapes of objects. The 20th-century "modern" artist goes one, even several steps beyond the traditions of the past because he makes the viewer work in a different way. In order to recognize the object the viewer must first experience something about it through the mind and emotions of the artist.

The subject of modern art is complicated—critics and historians do not agree on many things about it, how it started or what it means. The types of "modern" artists are so varied, their techniques so different, that whatever is said describes some but not all. At the turn of the century, artists were no longer content to copy. In looking for a new visual language they were expressing the feelings of a new age—an age of science, technology, machines, and structures like the Brooklyn Bridge.

Paris was the center of these art revolutions, and it was here that Stella found himself in 1911. He met Matisse and Picasso and became involved in the new art movements. How strange! He had gone back to Europe to study the art of the past—in Paris he confronted the future.

Two styles which especially appealed to him were Cubism and Futurism. When Stella first met the Cubists, he said he was so upset he could not paint for six months. What was Picasso doing? His paintings looked so mechanical, with sharp angles and grey and brown colors. Everything looked like broken or exploding cubes. The style was called "Cubism" and the painters "Cubists." Together they set the course of Western art in a new direction.

What did the Cubists see? They saw and painted things as they were—in three dimensions: width, length, and depth. The Cubist saw geometrical structure and patterns in all objects. Trees, mountains, furniture, all objects were combinations of geometrical shapes: cones, spheres, cubes, and so forth. The Cubists experimented with new ways of showing three dimensional objects on a two dimensional surface. In traditional paintings, painters had shown objects from one or two sides only. The Cubists sometimes included four or six sides: right and left, top, bottom, front and back. They painted objects such as chairs, tables, fruit in bowls, people, buildings and musical instruments, and depicted all sides, even the insides, at the same time. This was called the *principle of simultaneity.* We can't see all sides of an object at once, but the Cubist depicted all sides as visible simultaneously—that is, at the same time.

Albert Gleizes, one of the original Cubists, visited the United States and painted two Cubist style pictures of the Brooklyn Bridge. (page 26)

This is not a realistic representation. Gleizes chose the most recognizable parts, the network of cables, stays and suspenders, the arches, the buildings, and the headlights of cars at night. Then he rearranged them to dramatize the dynamic forces. With the curved lines of the cables sweeping upward, and the lines of the stays pointing downward, he created two strong opposing movements. In the overlapping angles and shapes, he causes the eye to move quickly from place to place. Across the middle, a row of circles inside other circles are like the glow of headlights at night driving straight at us. Above the noisy angles and shapes the arch rises majestic and strong. The buildings at the bottom of the painting represent Brooklyn and those at the top are in Manhattan. Gleizes has given us an interpretation of the bridge in the Cubist style instead of a representation. He rearranged the parts to emphasize the bridge's most dramatic and dynamic features. Joseph Stella used Cubist

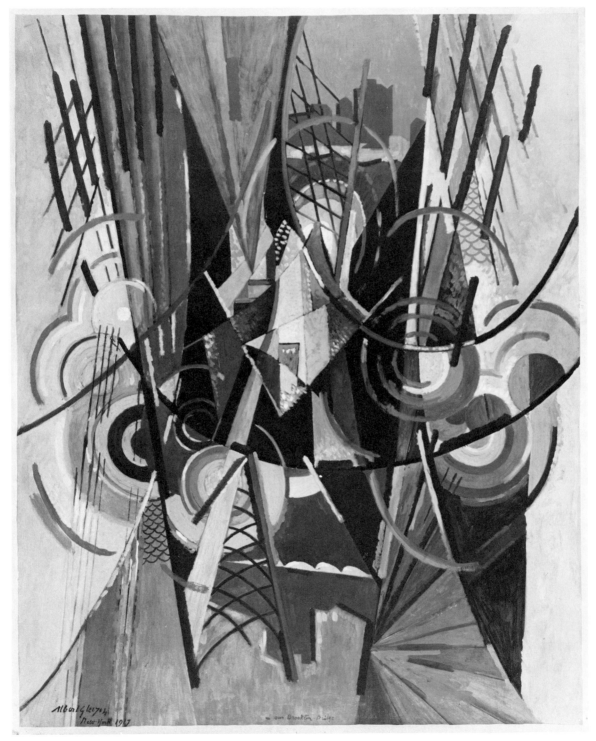

Albert Gleizes *On Brooklyn Bridge* (1917)

techniques with more restraint. Compare his painting (page 3) with Gleizes.

In the lower half of Stella's bridge, he applied the *principle of simultaneity* by showing us the under structure of the bridge at the same time that he shows us the front of the arches. On the left, he shows us the inner structure of the bridge. On the right, Stella shows us a long view of the roadway as it tapers to a point. Now, look at the full painting again. Notice how two sets of suspenders rise to the top of the arch. There Stella shows us a view of the bridge as it might look from the distance, without the towers. If we were standing in front of the arches, such views would be impossible. But a painter can create such views using the principle of simultaneity.

In the very beginning of the book we noted that one difference between a photograph and painting is that the artist is free to add what he wants. But the artist is not free from the laws and structure of his art. Both Gleizes and Stella made changes in the bridge to suit their designs. In the Gleizes work, notice how he curved the center of the tower instead of giving it the Gothic point. The curved arch repeats the curve of the circles and gives a visual harmony to the design by turning the eye downward instead of directing it up and off the page.

Look at the photograph of the bridge and locate the stays. Stella omitted them because this is a tall, thin painting. The diagonal stays would have broken the vertical motion of the angles and cubes. Each painter used Cubism in his own way. Each is free to break down different views of the bridge but he must fit the pieces together and lock them into a design that makes visual sense.

While in Italy Stella had become acquainted with another group of modern artists; in Paris he embraced their work. These were the Italian Futurists. The Futurists glorified the noise and speed of the new century. They painted the total city environment, including the sights, sounds, smells, speed and mechanization of modern civilization. Since sounds and smells are invisible, the Futurists invented *lines of force* that curve, twist, dash or cut across their paintings to show dynamic energy—great forces of movement. Both the Cubists and Futurists were responding to the Machine Age. They were interpreting the energy of the 20th century in their art. In 1911 Stella returned to the United States and experimented with Futurism. His bridge painted in 1918 shows the futurist technique.

Stella chose to paint the first of his six bridges "in the mysterious depth of night." Many nights he stood alone in the middle of the bridge feeling lost in the surrounding darkness. Memories of cold winter nights in Brooklyn depressed him. The mountainous skyscrapers of Manhattan seemed to crush him. The roar of the trains beneath him and the shrill voice of the trolley wires shook him. He heard the "strange moanings of appeal from the tugboats ... through the infernal recesses below." He felt, he said, "deeply moved, as if on the threshold of a new religion." For 20 years he had been obsessed by the bridge.

Finally Stella felt he had the technique and skills to say what he wanted to say about the bridge. Paris had given him the start. He had needed to find a way to express in paint the sounds of traffic and subways and the movement of lights. He had to learn to change a tower into a shrine or cathedral and to show the electric force and energy of the bridge. He learned how through Futurism. To express his vision, Stella needed a canvas larger than himself. It was seven-feet high and six-feet, four-inches wide. In 1918, the very size of the canvas was unusual.

This is a mysterious bridge. It is not a solid stone and steel cabled bridge. It is an illusion built of shrieking sounds and moving lights. It is a structure created by lines of force. Can you find them? They cut across the

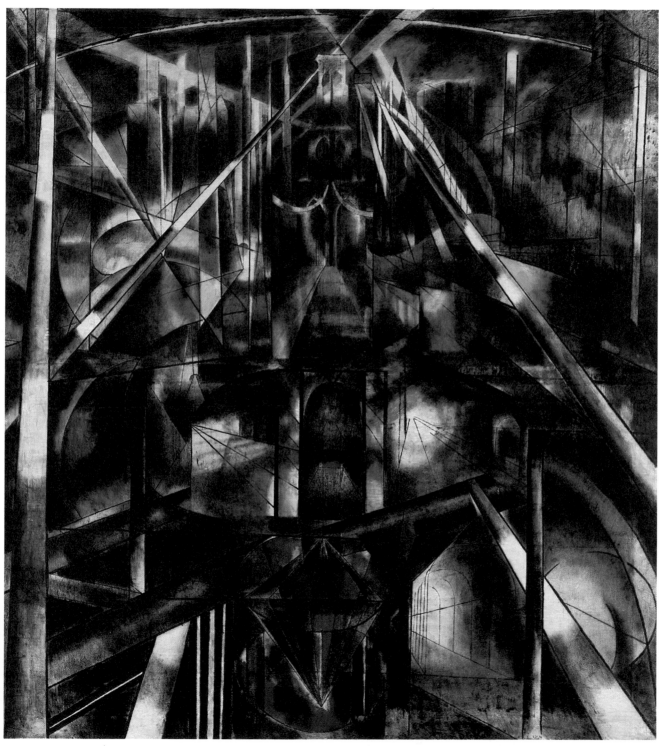

Joseph Stella *Brooklyn Bridge* (1917–1918)

face of the bridge like searchlights creating angles and triangles. They crisscross the upper sections like telegraph wires. They converge at points in the tunnels of the lower section. The colors flash over them like the lights of moving cars.

The Brooklyn Bridge has two towers, the Manhattan tower and the Brooklyn tower, but Stella painted three, one above the other. In this way, he glorified the towers and the Gothic arch. The two bottom towers are in the shadows. The top tower rises above the rest of the bridge, almost as high as the skyscrapers behind it. He recreated the bridge as an architectural structure like a cathedral or, as he said, ". . . as the shrine containing all the efforts of the new civilization of America." In this painting he created more than just a shrine. It was a whole cathedral. The top part creates a feeling of walking on Roebling's bridge. People passed through the high narrow Gothic arches raising heavenward. They looked up at the network of cables, stays, and suspenders. It was as if they were in a cathedral open to the sky and stars—a cathedral built to glorify stone, steel and industry. While painting it he said he appealed to the verses of Walt Whitman "I hear America singing; I hear America bringing builders—here is not really a nation, but a teeming nation among nations." Such verses found their symbol in the arches of the bridge.

If the top of the painting is religious, the lower part is the darker side of America. What was this dark side of America that Stella struggled with so much and where is it in the painting? Look again at the painting of the bridge on page 29. Notice the red glow in the diamond shape. You will also find a red glow in his other paintings of the bridge, often in the tunnels.

What is the red glow? Is it just a light? The critic Irma Jaffe found similar red glows in the smoke stacks of his factory drawings. She suggests the red glow comes from his memory of Mount Vesuvius, the volcano near his home in Italy. It is the lava boiling. It is also the red molten steel in vats of steel mills, the red fires powering engines. Perhaps Stella was showing us his memory of the tragic deaths in the Monogah mine disasters— where an entire village of mine workers was buried alive.

Hidden in the depths of the bridge is something Stella might not have known he was painting. Perhaps it was another way his mind found to express his feeling about the two sides of the American dream: death and destruction within progress and industry. Look carefully at the round Roman arch, the tunnels on each side of it and the diamond shape below it. The arch is like the hollow nose of a skull, the two tunnels its eye sockets and the diamond shape its teeth. The drawing below will help you see it.

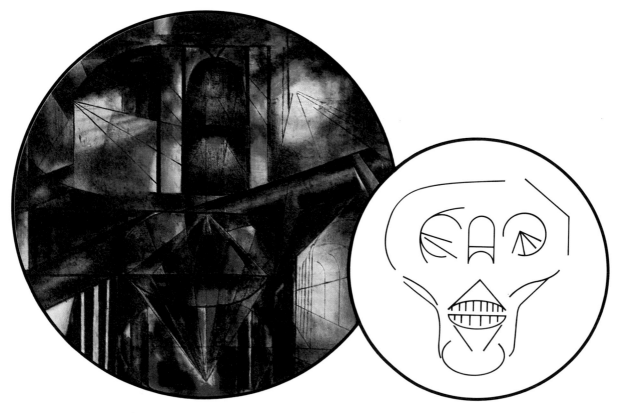

The head of death hidden in the painting is a reminder of the deaths of immigrants in mine disasters, factories and the building of the bridge. In this first painting Stella described the glory of America's engineering and industry and the tragedy he found in the cost of human lives to achieve such accomplishments.

Soon after he completed this painting, Stella began his major work, *Voice of the City, New York Interpreted.* This is a series of five paintings arranged geographically around Manhattan: (1) *The Port;* (2) *White Way I;* (3) *The Skyscrapers;* (4) *White Way II;* and (5) *The Bridge.* The five paintings together are impressions of the speed, sounds and constant motion of city life. Stella intended *New York Interpreted* as his major work and added drama by writing flowery descriptions of each panel. As you look at the panels, do Stella's words add to the meaning?

The Port. "You have reached the harbor; you are standing where all the arteries of the great giant

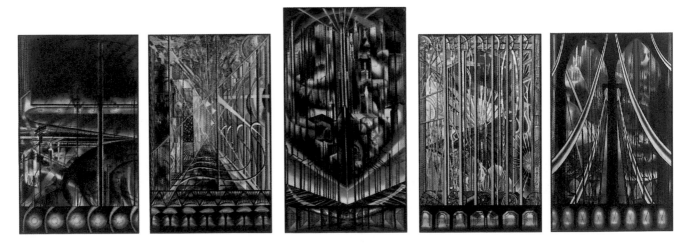

Joseph Stella *Voice of the City: New York Interpreted*
The Port -White Way I - The Skyscrapers - White Way II - The Bridge (1922)

meet; and a quiet sea and sky overwhelm you; you have left the noise and glare of Broadway; all the hardness and brilliancy fade away in the stillness of the night."

The Port (New York Harbor) has more open space than the other four panels. There is a spiritual feeling in the blue-greens of the dark sky and sea. In the upper left, he painted a row of smokestacks to "rise like a triumphant song of a new religion"—the religion of industry. Below them, among telegraph poles and storage tanks, the factories are hidden in darkness. The port is quiet, dark, mysterious. It is night. Only a few distant ships move across the silent water.

White Way I. "Here are some sensations produced by the confusion of light and sound as one emerges from subterranean passages to the streets above.
" White Way II another interpretation of the sensations produced by the confusion in the streets."

The "Great White Way" was a popular name for the theater district on Broadway around Times Square. The brilliant white lights on marquees and billboards seem to form a bright and glittering road leading to the stars and for some, to stardom. In contrast to *The Port,* these panels are ablaze with brilliant light. They sparkle with the laughter and jewels of the theater district, with the neon nightlife of Manhattan. *White Way I* clamors with sounds and lights.

The Skyscrapers "An interpretation of the city's colossal skyscrapers blended together in a symphony of lights in the shape of a high vessel's prow."

All the panels are the same height except *The Sky-scrapers.* By making it the tallest and the central panel, Stella made it dominate the other panels, just as the skyscrapers dominate the city. They make everything seem small, even the Brooklyn Bridge. *The Skyscrapers* is symmetrical with the buildings coming together in the center to form the prow of a ship. The shape of the buildings suggest the Flatiron Building, a narrow triangular structure that was one of the tallest in New York City when Stella made this painting. The real buildings were constructed of stone and steel. They are not Stella's thin, light, airy skyscrapers. What have we then? Stella, in his fantasy city, had a prophetic vision. He created buildings anticipating those of today. Stella's are the steel glass-mirrored walls of today's buildings. His is a vision of a city to come in which the buildings float row upon row.

The Bridge. "An abstract representation of that engineering epic in steel. A sinewed span of human energy." This is Stella's bridge of 1922 that we looked at earlier.

Although part of *New York Interpreted,* it is a complete painting by itself. From the position on the extreme right it towers over the city. It is there, a haven from the hectic motion of life below in the other panels. In its solid symmetry you feel the calm of Stella's night. Of all the panels, *The Bridge* is the most popular.

At the bottom of the five panels is a border, called a *predella.* Notice how it extends across each panel, with a similar design—a row of ovals, circles, and arches. They represent the subways and tunnels which criss-cross under New York City and the rivers on each side of Manhattan. The spoked wheel and hubcap shapes represent the thousands of trains, trucks and automobiles that drive through these tunnels day and night. The predella helps tie all five panels together into a single design.

The choice of the number of panels tells something about Stella's intentions for his work. Five panels make a *polyptych.* A polyptych was a small altar piece used in Italian churches during the Middle Ages. At the bottom of the polyptych was the predella. Although his city resembles a ship, it has the feel of a gigantic cathedral. But inside the cathedral is a hotbed of commotion. This is not traditional religion, nor is it traditional art. It is religion of the 20th century—the age of the machine, science, technology, and of millions of people thrown together in cramped space. There are no people in Stella's city, but it is full of human emotions. We see life whirling around at indescribable speeds and ferocious energy. The effect is what Stella wanted—it is dizzying. His vertical city pushes ever upward to unlimited heights and goals. But once inside, the constant repetition of vertical lines feels more like the bars of a prison. Is *New York Interpreted* a cathedral, a prison, or both? Look again and decide.

Although there are enough modern styles to fill volumes, *New York Interpreted* is considered America's most important futurist work. In it Stella used lines of force to unify the five panels into one large painting, and to show energy, light, and movement inside each sepa-

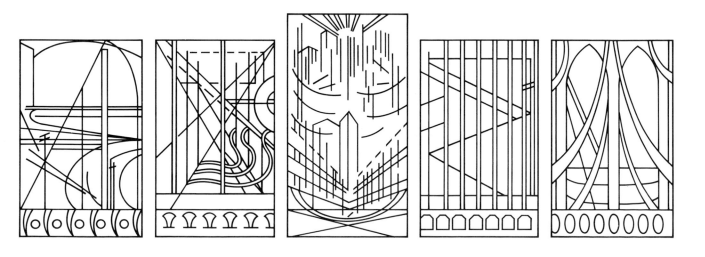

rate panel. Go to the painting and find lines of force. Then go to the drawing which shows some of these lines of force. The major diagonal and curved lines move your eye past the verticals to the other panels. Look back at the pictures on page 32 and find some lines of force not in the drawings. Notice, also, the vertical curves in *The Bridge* on the right. They stop your eye and hold it inside the panel. When looking at the panels from left to right, *the last panel is like a giant exclamation mark at the end of a sentence!*

Stella went on to do four more paintings of the bridge. He returned again to Italy and France where he lived from 1929 to 1934. In Paris an important exhibit was being planned. Stella wanted one of his paintings of the bridge in the show, but there was not enough time to have it shipped to him. So, he painted another bridge in 1929.

Stella called it *American Landscape.* But what kind of landscape is it? Where are the trees? The hills? It is a vertical landscape of buildings, factories, warehouses, and bridges. Compare this painting with the first two bridges. Compare the buildings. How are they different? These buildings are solid. They do not float on clouds. They are more like a wall. The buildings are grey and black with shafts of blue, red, and green. The suspenders of the bridge are wider, more like the iron bars of a closed gate. Again, below the bridge are the firey red arches. Where are we as we look at this bridge? What is our point of view? We are not on the bridge, but off to one side. The bridge is left of center. The sweeping curve of cables crosses over our vision to block our view. We are kept outside.

Stella painted this bridge from memory on the other side of the Atlantic Ocean. It is no longer an open door; it is a closed gate. Although Stella glorified New York City in his painting, he was never at home here. As an

Joseph Stella *American Landscape* (1929)

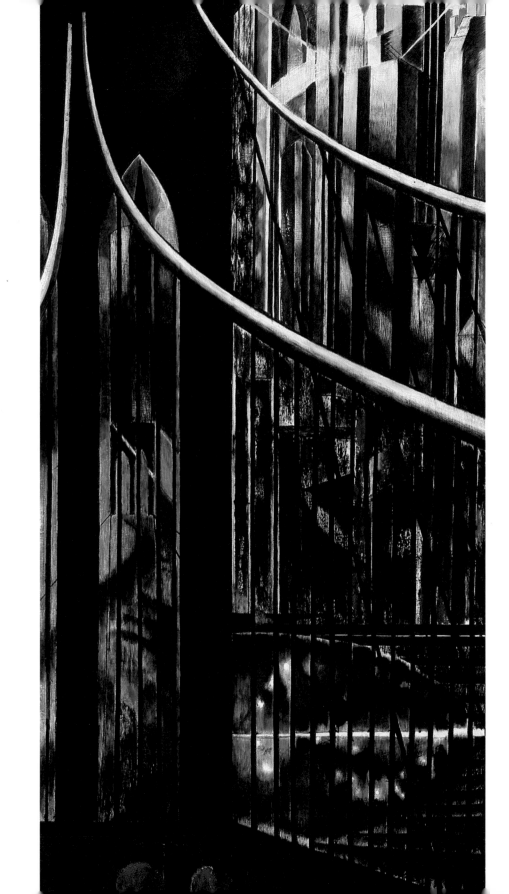

immigrant, he felt he was an outsider. This bridge is a barrier to the city. He is outside looking in. Yet, when he was inside, the walls of the city seemed like a prison. He never really felt at home in Europe or America.

The style of this third bridge came from still another art movement in the United States. Again, American artists were responding to the machine and industrialization. But instead of painting the effect of industry on people's lives, they glorified the machine itself. They were called the *Precisionists* because they painted geometrically precise pictures of smooth-surfaced machinery, buildings, bridges, and interiors. They simplified objects, cleaned them of all textures and details. The machinery was painted as if brand new with no rust, grime, or sooted surfaces. They painted new machines for a new century, a new age. The Precisionists usually did not include people, flowers, or nature in their paintings. Industry was making the United States a world power. It was this the Precisionists celebrated. This was the new American landscape that Stella celebrated with his industrial landscape.

Stella's fourth painting of the bridge in 1936 was a simplified version of his second. In this work the lower structure is gone, and there is no second bridge in the right arch. The buildings are straighter and plainer. Something else has happened. The mysterious threatening darkness of the first bridges has been replaced by a mist.

Three years later in 1939, Stella returned to the color and drama of the *New York Interpreted* bridge. He called it *Brooklyn Bridge: Variations on an Old Theme* because he repeated certain symbols and designs from the *New York Interpreted* panels. These skyscrapers are more solid than his earlier ones. By 1939 the buildings in New York City were getting taller and more like Stella's prophetic vision. Here, Stella's buildings stand on a row of arches instead of floating on the clouds of smoke and

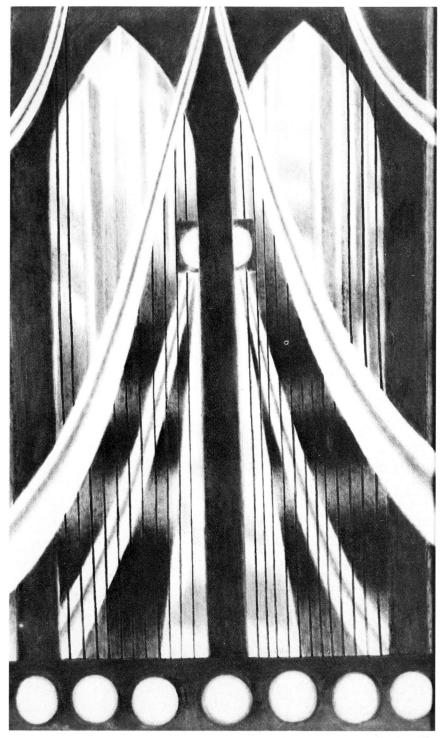

Joseph Stella *The Bridge* (1936)

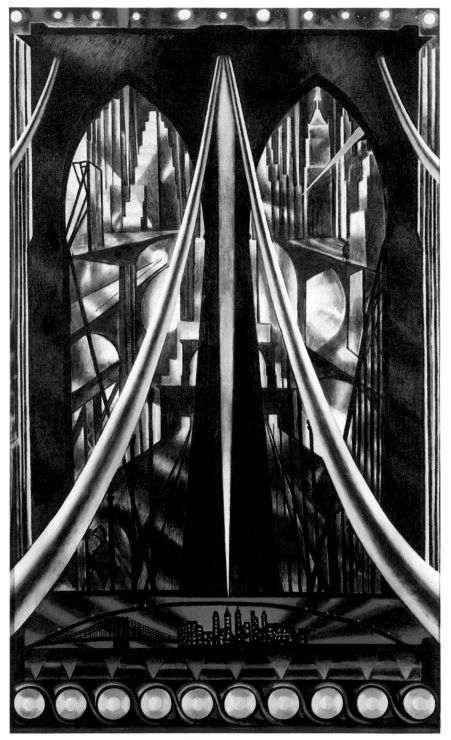

Joseph Stella *Brooklyn Bridge, Variations on an Old Theme* (1939)

mist of the earlier painting. On a platform in the upper-left section, the frame of a single flat for a stage set stands alone. It is the theater district with the light of *White Way I.* This tower has space and stars around it. Rays of light project from the skyscrapers to the stars. Strips of bright yellow border the sides of the tower. The roadway is open. Blues and yellows replace the dark mystery of the subways and tunnels.

Stella painted his last bridge in 1941 when he was 63.

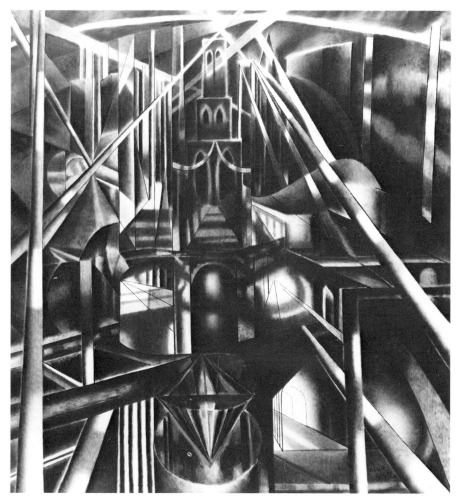

Joseph Stella *The Old Bridge* (1941)

He called it *The Old Bridge.* It is almost exactly like the first one he painted 23 years earlier when he was 41 years old. Compare both versions. *The Old Bridge* has the same basic design, but Stella simplified it. Notice how he removed some of the lines cutting across the surface of the painting—especially in the upper and lower right corners. There are fewer tiny shapes in the tunnels and lower half. The buildings and bridge structures are more solid.

Stella died in 1946. He has a permanent place in the history of American art as our leading Futurist. He had no students to carry on his ideas. But his paintings of the Brooklyn Bridge inspired other artists and writers to see it as a symbol of the American dream, a cathedral, a collection of force and energy, as a gateway to a new world.

There are now countless paintings of the Brooklyn Bridge. Roebling gave us a gift—a bridge of many meanings. It was itself a work of art. For Roebling it represented the perfect balance of natural forces at rest, a perfect merger of architecture in the stone towers and engineering in the steel ropes, cables and riverspan. Each artist finds his or her own meanings and turns them into art.

But Joseph Stella showed us a bridge of ever-changing meaning. Under the spell of the bridge, Stella painted it as three different symbols. Each one represented a part of himself. Each reveals another part of his obsession. The first was a cathedral—to express his spiritual search and exaltation. The second was an open gateway to the city, welcoming him as an outsider, the eternal immigrant. The third was the closed door locking him out. The next two paintings repeated the gateway bridge, and the last painting, *The Old Bridge,* was almost a copy of his first bridge—the cathedral, the shrine to the "Civilization of America."

Under his obsession with the Brooklyn Bridge, Stella opened our eyes to the possibilities as well as to the satisfactions of modern art. But what does it mean when an artist says he had "an obsession with a bridge"? Obsessions, like passions, have no logic or reasonable answers. They come from the human heart and defy explanations.

The paintings of the bridges shed some light on this mysterious obsession and offer a clue to the relationship between an artist and his work. Go back again and look at his six different paintings of the bridge. Even as they are different how are they the same?

His first bridge is considered a "Futurist" bridge. But it really is not a Futurist painting. Futurist paintings glorified speed and consisted of restless motion. Stella's first bridge has motion, but it also has stability. The second bridge has even more. In this second one—his most famous—the heavy weight of the structure frames— even holds down—the activity. In all six paintings even as the bridge soars, it is as solid as steel and stone. Although Stella rejected the Futurists there is reason to understand his fascination with them. Futurists glorified the speed and motion of modern life. Stella's own life was filled with restless motion. He had come to the United States as a young man, when the bridge was but 14 years old. With his own eyes he witnessed the explosion of New York into what he called the "imperial city" of the 20th century. Stella loved his city, but he never really felt at home here, or anywhere else for that matter. He was an immigrant in New York, and a wanderer in life. Several times he went from New York to Europe and back again. Throughout his life, this restless man wandered between countries just as he wandered between different styles of art. In his later years he mastered modern art, yet he continued to make lovely portraits in the style of the Old Masters.

In the big paintings of the bridge, Stella chose "abstract" art. Perhaps only in this style could he describe and make visual sense out of the towering city and the restless rush of modern urban life. But in making "visual sense" out of it all, he gave the bridges the stability and calm he never had in his own life. The bridges, closed or open, exits or entrances, reveal much about this man on the move, this 20th-century nomad, this unhappy bird of flight in search of his cage. In his paintings of New York and its Brooklyn Bridge we see his personal turmoil in the chaos of modern life. But we also feel how Stella imposed order on all this chaos. If we experienced the bridge through the mind of the modern artist, we can feel his emotions and peer into his heart. Is this just a wild idea? For who really knows the reasons for obsessions or why the artist paints. But the evidence is there: a restless life at peace under the solid frame of the bridge.

His different paintings of the bridge opened up new ways of seeing the triumph and tragedy of the American landscape. All the artists who give us their different views of the bridge opened up new ways of seeing the world as well as ourselves. We look at these bridges not knowing if they are entrances or exits. The very act of entering a new place means leaving an old one. This bridge and all bridges are roads that rise above barriers in our way. We all build our own bridges, but along the way the river gods demand sacrifice. When a human being makes sacrifices it is called growing up. When the river is sacrificed to the bridge it is called progress. Roebling sacrificed his life to a gateway to the future, and to a bridge between the 19th and 20th centuries. Joseph Stella's sacrifice was a life marked by his uneasy obsession with a bridge. But this obsession was only part of a bigger obsession—the obsession to paint it. In his art he changed the view of the landscape. As in the ancient myths, he made his sacrifice and paid his price. But the wanderer's achievement stands as solid as the bridge.

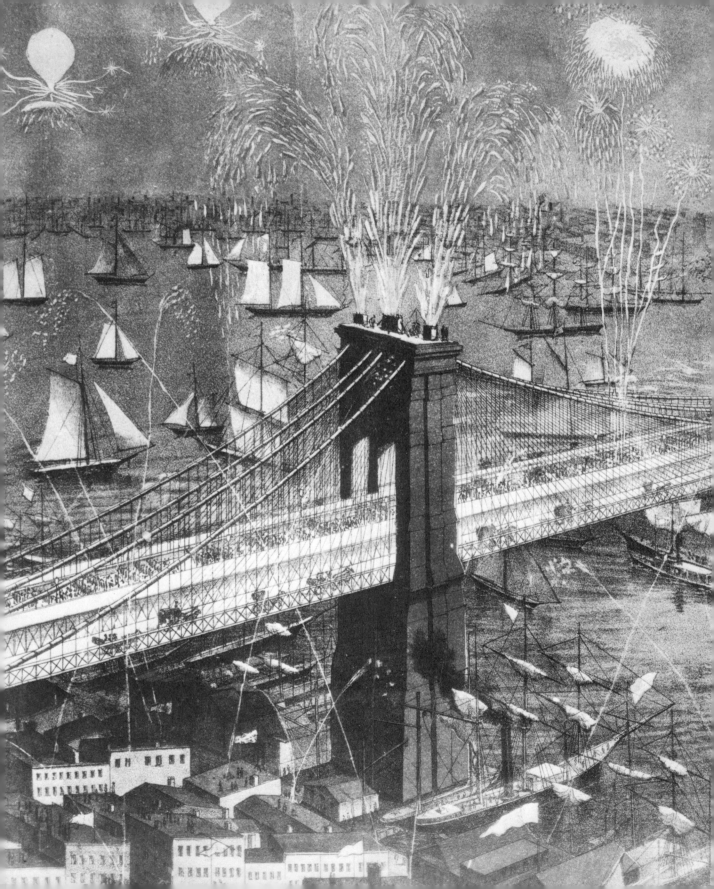